# Confessions of a Weaver

By Sherrie Amada Miller

© 2013 Sherrie Amada Miller
All Rights Reserved.

Illustrations by Mark Hill

No part of this publication may be reproduced, stored in a retrieval system, or transmitted, in any form or by any means, electronic, mechanical,
photocopying, recording, or otherwise, without the written permission of
the author.

First published by Dog Ear Publishing
4010 W. 86th Street, Ste H
Indianapolis, IN 46268
www.dogearpublishing.net

ISBN: 978-1-4575-2073-0

This book is printed on acid-free paper.

Printed in the United States of America

# Dedication

This book is dedicated to my husband who thinks everything I weave is wonderful.

# Forward

*A* romp of a good read...I smiled through the entire book. Storytelling is part of our cultural roots and finding a good story teller that grabs the essence of the passion of handweaving and tells those stories in such a personal and spirited way makes *Confessions of a Weaver* a jewel in every weaver's library. In reality, all fiber enthusiasts will find something to sing about in these pages as Miller touches on the passions and pitfalls of a fiber obsession. She writes about her "dogged determination" to stick with a project, and her failures and triumphs in a humorous and entertaining way. The occasional illustration by Mark Hill that accompanies some of these charming personal essays gives the reader an additional reason to smile.

I've known Sherrie Miller for many years as a friend and fellow guild mate. She wove many beautiful inspired garments for the color forecast columns I wrote for *Handwoven Magazine/Interweave Press*. Sherrie is unassuming and self-effacing yet whenever she would present a show and tell for the guild, there was always a great story that would accompany her woven treasure.

*Confessions of a Weaver* is the kind of book you curl up with in the afternoon, with a warm cup of tea, the cat in your lap, and baskets of colorful yarn at your side.

Daryl Lancaster

Former Features Editor *Handwoven Magazine*
Author, Educator, Handweaver

# Introduction

*D*id you ever start to weave something that you thought would be beautiful and watch in horror as it turned into one of the ugliest things to ever come off your loom? Do you have a large collection of unfinished projects tucked away in your weaving room? Have you ever been frustrated because the fiber you absolutely must have for a project is on back order, or worse, has been discontinued? If you can relate to any of these situations, then come along with me as I confess all in *Confessions of a Weaver*. This is a weaver's companion book that explores with humor the emotions and thoughts engendered by an intense relationship with weaving. Even though most of us weave alone, hopefully you'll relate to my personal essays and feel the bond that weavers share.

# My True Confession

*I*'ve often wondered if I am the only adult with this most unusual habit. Like all confessions, there is some shame inherent in my story. I know my parents, particularly my mother, was always embarrassed by it. The earliest evidence of it is recorded in a photo album from our family outing to Bear Mountain State Park in New York.

I was around three years old then and appear to be having a good time with my father. He holds my hand as we walk down a wide path, steadies me as I walk along the top of a stone wall and lifts me up for a view of the Hudson River. These are sweet black and white souvenirs of an innocent time past. I'm wearing a classic little girl dress with puffy sleeves and a Peter Pan collar, but what in the world is hanging from my hand? In almost every photo, I'm holding onto something that wouldn't be obvious to anyone who didn't know me as a child.

Sixty-plus years later I have no memory of this pleasant excursion, a change of scenery for sure from our home in Newark, NJ. But I absolutely know what I was holding in my hand. It was my security blanket—not actually a blanket, but an old sweater that my mother had knit for me as a baby. Before I learned to say the word "sweater," I called it my "wetter" and my happiness depended on it.

My mother was probably horrified that I was dragging an old raggedy sweater around in public. She thought a child sucking a pacifier was a disgraceful sight. A child picking at the tattered remains of a woolen sweater was just as bad and maybe even worse. Children need to hold their security blankets, whether they're actual blankets, stuffed animals or toys. My particular path to security wasn't dependent on just holding or cuddling something soft; I needed something wooly to pick.

Having a mother who was an extraordinary knitter, I probably started life wrapped in hand knit woolen blankets and sweaters. At some point I must have discovered that it was pleasurable to pick at wool and pull out little loose bits of fiber. Who needed a pacifier? When life got stressful, I found that rubbing those little loose fibers against my cuticles calmed me down and felt surprisingly good. Only wool had this magic power.

My mother could tell if I was picking, as in, "Sherrie, stop picking!" by looking at my face. She claimed my mouth changed shape as I picked and my eyes got a faraway look. Maybe this was OK for a baby, but not a big girl. (Has anyone else in the world ever turned their cuticles and fingertips into pleasure zones?) Picking felt so good I saw no reason to stop it. Compared to thumb sucking, which is hard to hide, this was something I could do surreptitiously. And I did.

Mothers may not have eyes in the back of their heads, but they don't miss much. My mother knew that I never outgrew the habit she viewed as both infantile and disturbing. My beloved old sweater had fallen apart years ago, but ordinary woolen sweaters and jackets worked just as well. Even if I picked when no one was watching, there were always telltale fuzzy patches where my picking had pulled out lots of little wooly fibers.

When I was around eight years old, my mother made me a proposal; if I would stop picking she would buy me a special present. I could choose whatever I wanted. This was a dangerous proposition but she was desperate. Since there was something I really wanted, I agreed to her bargain. I would trade picking for a merry-go-round. The best part of our summer vacations in Asbury Park, even better than going to the beach, was riding the iconic merry-go-round on the boardwalk pavilion. No matter how many rides my parents paid for, it was never enough. Both my mother and I were happy with our agreement and I promised to stop picking as soon as I got a merry-go-round.

Some promises need to be clarified. We both understood that I was swearing off picking in return for a merry-go-round, but we had very different merry-go-rounds in mind. One afternoon with great excitement my mother handed me a large box. "Here it is," she happily proclaimed and I eagerly tore open the box, unprepared for its contents. It was a toy merry-go-round. I looked at it with disgust. "This isn't what I wanted," I complained. "This is just a toy. I wanted a *real* merry-go-round."

As bright and charming as it was, I had no use for that merry-go-round and I certainly wasn't going to give up picking for it. If I couldn't have the real thing, our deal was off. My mother was deeply disappointed. I felt as if I had been cheated and dealt with my unhappiness the best way I knew, by picking.

From my mother's point of view, aside from the picking habit, I seemed to be a normal little girl. I played with dolls, enjoyed my dancing lessons and played games on our front steps with a pink rubber ball. What I liked the most though, was "making things." My mother taught me how to knit and I made doll blankets. Every family member received a colorful potholder that I wove on my classic potholder loom. I loved making what we called "horse reins" back then on a little spool with nails. My mother, the woman who could knit the back of a sweater in a dark movie theater, understood the pleasure of making things. She saw possibilities for a revised trade-off.

A few months after the merry-go-round fiasco my mother decided to try again. She asked if there was something else I would like instead. I was stretching loops on my metal frame when she asked. By now I was tired of weaving on my potholder loom and noticed that none of the potholder recipients seemed very excited anymore. When my mother asked what she could buy me this time, I had an answer. I wanted a real loom. I had probably seen a simple rigid heddle type loom somewhere. So we struck another deal: a real loom in return for my promise to stop picking. A real loom was a much easier request. Neither my mother nor I had ever seen a multi-harness loom back in 1950. Any piece of equipment that could turn yarn into woven fabric (as opposed to knitting) was a real loom.

My mother, delighted with her easy new mission, immediately bought me a rigid heddle loom. This time I was satisfied. The loom was made from light wood and came pre-warped with that classic variegated bright yarn that appeals to children. Today when I look at the Harrisville Easy Weaver loom, I'm reminded of my first real loom. If mine wasn't an actual Easy Weaver, it was very similar in design. I loved it! My mother had kept her promise and now I was going to keep mine.

I really tried to keep my promise to stop picking. Looking back I don't remember how long I lasted. Maybe I was able to fight off the urge for a month or so, but the need to pick eventually overpowered my resolve to give it up. Feeling guilty, I did it in secret. Maybe that was good enough for my mother. If she couldn't see me doing it, than no one else could either.

Now here comes my true confession. I still pick. I never was able to wean myself away from woolen fabric. The feel of those little woolen fibers on my cuticles is just as pleasurable today as it was when I was three years old. The downside is that many of my woolen sweaters and jackets have areas that are a bit worn or fuzzy. And sometimes my cuticles look a little ragged. Since my first real loom I've never even thought about quitting and don't plan to. I actually feel quite fortunate. While other people need a glass of wine or a cigarette to relax and unwind, I just need to touch something with woolen fibers. What an appropriate addiction for a weaver.

# Ménage à Trois

*I* feel sorry for my husband. He thinks we're a couple but we're not. We're really a threesome. There's my husband, there's me and then there's my Loom. It's the relationship with The Loom that's the problem, but I haven't figured out yet who's to blame. A psychologist would immediately recognize that The Loom is the dominant one in this trio. It has the power to influence my moods. When everything on my loom is going well I am a calm and happy person. I'm easy to live with and readily shrug off annoyances and irritants. When my loom throws a weaving tantrum, I become obsessed with finding and fixing the problem. It's the only thing I can focus on. Nothing else matters. Normal daily life comes to a halt for all of us.

It's a good thing I don't have dependent children still living at home. They would starve while waiting for me to locate and fix nasty threading errors. When crossed threads make my blood pressure rise and dinner time rolls around, I wish I was eligible for Meals on Wheels. How can I possibly cook dinner knowing I'm missing three warp ends? I am so driven that if the White House secretary called to tell me that the President wanted to speak with me, I would ask if he could call back later.

The Loom has an uncanny way of choosing inopportune times to demand my attention. It seems to sense when I've made a commitment to be with my husband. The day the Netflix movie that my husband and I have been waiting for finally arrives, for instance. We agree to start watching it at 8:00 pm. Between dinner and our movie date, I have about an hour to finish warping my floor loom and then begin weaving a waffle-weave baby blanket for our newest granddaughter. I picture her wrapped in my soft handwoven blanket and feel happy. I love being a weaver.

Three weft shots later a diabolical threading error reveals itself. It's now 7:50 pm. As my husband reminds me that it's almost time to start watching the movie, I begin to sweat. All I want to do is fix the mess on my loom. I need to penetrate the forest of heddles strung out before me and slowly and methodically hunt down the guilty warp ends. I need time. I cannot relax until my warp is repaired. It's now 8:00 pm and I can hear my husband starting up the DVD. He's ready to watch the movie and doesn't realize how painfully aware I am of the hour. Like a town crier, he calls out the time in case I haven't noticed. It is 8:00 pm and all is not well. I am trapped between The Loom and my husband in an emotional tug of war.

Most of the time my husband wins. My feelings of guilt over all the time I spend alone with the loom gives him a decided edge. Like a sullen child, I silently join him in the family room and together we start watching the movie. As I get caught up in the drama of the movie the loom drama fades away. I'm glad I was forced out of the weaving room. While munching a bowl of freshly popped popcorn, I regain perspective. Would I really have preferred spending my evening alone fighting with fiber? The messed-up warp will still be there tomorrow.

Being part of this threesome can be tricky. Weaving is a solitary activity and comes with its own unique timekeeping system. Minutes don't exist in a weaving zone. Everything takes hours, days, weeks, months or even longer to complete. Projects get finished when they're finished. Ironically, time seems to speed up in my weaving room. Every time I glance at the clock, it's always much later than I imagined. While I've worked at my loom, entire weekends have come and gone.

Will my husband start feeling like a weaving widower? Will he begin to resent having an absentee wife and sharing his home with eight looms? (Four are for my weaving students!) A weaving acquaintance once confessed to me that her husband refused to let her bring her loom into the house. I don't know what caused him to make such a dire edict, but he is now her ex-husband.

A ménage à trois takes some delicate balancing. Sometimes I feel like a husband trying to keep a wife and mistress happy at the same time. So far I have all the spousal support any weaver could wish for. My husband's excellent mechanical abilities have saved many a weaving day and he appreciates my woven output. Like lava, the overflow from my weaving room has worked its way into almost every room of our house, but that doesn't bother him. Even the extra looms permanently parked in the family room, dining room and guest room are not a problem. I can think of only one thing that would upset the equilibrium of our threesome. No matter what cataclysmic fiber event occurs in my weaving room, I better be ready for our 8:00 pm movie dates.

# Do You Recognize this Warning Sign?

*I* have a friend who enjoys cleaning. She is the only one I ever met who feels that way. For me, cleaning is something to put off until you have no choice. It takes a lot of cat hair and dust before I feel the need to do anything about it. The ultimate motivator of course is knowing that someone will be coming over. Up until now I've managed to hide my extremely high threshold for living with dusty furniture and cat hair tumbleweeds. I have to feel impending shame and grave embarrassment to convince me it's time to clean.

Yesterday, out of the blue, I got an urge to clean my weaving room. In addition to the usual dusty mix, the floor was covered with a rainbow of lint and threads. Under my Mighty Wolf floor loom a thick layer of colored fuzz, ghosts from past weaving projects, was undoubtedly creating air quality rivaling that of L.A. smog. If I were a spinner, I bet I could have carded and spun some of that debris into an interesting yarn.

I dragged the vacuum into my weaving room and started cleaning the rug under the loom. The before and after appearance of the floor was such an improvement that I got inspired to hunt down more dirt. Before I knew it, I found myself actually dusting the cones of 5/2 pearl cotton lined up on a shelf. After running my swiffer duster around a few cones, something made me abruptly stop. What was I doing and why was I dusting cones of fiber? No guest was due to stop over. If I truly had an urge to clean, there was an ample supply of dirt in more conspicuous places.

My weaving room certainly looked more inviting. But why had I just spent an hour cleaning under every treadle, vacuuming all moving parts of my loom, reorganizing the forgotten pile of project ideas and as a grand finale, dusting cones of fiber? Then I realized what was happening.  Here was a classic case of "avoidance" cleaning.

The easiest tasks take little or no creative thought. Pay the bills, register for an adult school class, go to the gym or mail a package to a grandchild. These are straightforward and easy to cross off a to-do list. It's when my mental to-do list includes designing a new and hopefully exciting weaving project that I turn to avoidance cleaning.

I've been thinking about weaving fabric for a poncho ever since *Handwoven Magazine* had its poncho contest a few years ago. By the time I finally get around to designing and weaving yardage, I'm sure they'll be out of style again. I just can't seem to move beyond a vague concept stage. My loom is empty, waiting for a warm wooly poncho warp, but all I want to do is clean. When I can't face the challenge of starting a new project or figuring out how to solve a nasty problem, there's nothing as satisfying as avoidance cleaning. Vacuuming my window treatments and using a Q-tip to clean cat hair from heating ducts isn't going to get me any closer to a fashionable poncho, but it has turned procrastination from a bad habit into a real asset. If I can't come up with something soon, my entire house will be dust and cat hair-free.

# How to Go from Beautiful to Ugly Without Even Trying

All new weaving projects start out as interesting ideas. Inspired by a fiber, an intriguing color combination, a weave structure or an existing textile, I begin to mentally plan and execute a piece. Weaving thoughts and threads together in one's head is always exciting. Like a NASA rocket ready for launch, all creative systems are go and I can already imagine how beautiful this new piece will be. Maybe *Handwoven Magazine* will want it for an upcoming issue. Maybe it will be a bestseller at our guild sale in the fall. Won't it be fun to bring it to the next guild meeting for show and tell? This may be the best thing to ever come off my loom. The dream machine is hard to shut off.

Finally it's time to transform my inspired concept into fiber reality. With high spirits I merrily face my warping board and start measuring out warp with great enthusiasm. The colors look happy together and it's easy to follow the color sequence I charted out. This project requires over 500 warp ends, but winding the yarn around and around those pegs creates an easy, pleasant rhythm. Time doesn't matter. I no longer have to think as my arms on autopilot zigzag across the warping board's pegs.

The threading pattern is straightforward. It's only after I finished threading all 525 heddles that the first hint of uncertainty sneaks up on me. I dismiss it. With all of my years of weaving I should know by now what will work. This is going to be a wonderful textile. I'm close to bringing my creative vision to life.

The warp winds itself on without a single complaint and at last I'm ready to weave. Let the good times roll! I've put a lot of yardage on that rear beam, enough to keep me weaving for a long time.

An inch or so into the weaving I'm wondering when the magic will happen. I check my weft color sequence and double-check the draft's treadling. I'm definitely on track with my master plan but the beautiful fabric I've envisioned is nowhere to be found. What's wrong?

It's time to eat some humble pie. Even light-years of weaving experience cannot guarantee immunity from making something hideous. Many of my beautiful weaving dreams have produced certifiably ugly woven landscapes. I'm sure my fiber future holds yet more disasters. It's a remarkably short trip from beautiful fabric that makes you feel happy all day to fabric that makes you feel sick, really sick. I'm still amazed at the negative power of the wrong color choice, the wrong fibers, the wrong sett or the wrong weave structure. Somehow these are always the projects with yards and yards of warp waiting on the back beam and hundreds of warp ends neatly lined up in their heddles waiting for treadle action.

Of course hindsight always screams at me, "Why didn't you sample first? You even do samples for your guild's six inch swatch exchanges. Yet you didn't take this idea out for a test run before winding on six yards of warp?" Hindsight can be such an annoying smarty-pants but I am guilty as charged.
There is a definite philosophical fork in the road ahead. On one side is a long path to character building. It is strewn with punishment, frustration, aesthetic pain and suffering. Choosing this path is a vote for not giving up, for trying every option right through to Plan Z. Renouncing this warp is just irresponsible. Only a quitter (and we know how lacking in character a quitter is) would abandon this project.

The other path brings a different kind of distress. It's a much shorter road with one quick sharp pain, like that of pulling off a Band-Aid. Choosing that side of the fork gives me permission to cut the offending warp off the loom. A reassuring voice keeps telling me that there's no point in sticking with something that's doomed. Just cut it all off and forget it. The voice tells me that my character is good enough and there's no shame in making a mistake now and then.

I've reached that fork so many times. There are endless variations of ugliness, but my mental anguish is always the same. To avoid going into my weaving room, I sometimes resort to "avoidance cleaning" (see "Do You Recognize this Warning Sign?"). At that point I know it's time to make a decision. Even though I feel I've saved up more than enough character building to last for the foreseeable future, each and every time I invariably make the same decision. I always decide not to forsake the offensive warp.

So I go back to the loom with a revised set of goals. Forgetting about making something extraordinary, I'm just hoping to weave something I can stand looking at, something I can find a use for, any kind of use. Something that will give me sufficient incentive to stay at the loom long enough to weave off that endless warp rolled up on the back beam.

Now feeling released from any predetermined idea or plan, I try to view this as an opportunity to experiment with unexpected wefts. There must be something in my fiber repository to cheer up this sad project and me as well. Sometimes I can talk myself into thinking that my piece of weaving isn't really that awful. I know how a weaver can be her own worst critic. I muster up some weak enthusiasm to keep me going and going and going. I feel as if I'm the sorry maiden in a fairy tale, where the warp just keeps growing on the back beam no matter how often I advance my weaving. There's no prince in sight either.

By the time the back apron rod makes an appearance, I know I've accumulated a whole new batch of character building points. It's as if I have millions of frequent flyer miles, too many to use up in one lifetime. How much character do I need? Did I make the right decision at that tricky fork in the road?

With a tentative spurt of optimism, I unroll my fabric, hoping for some sort of miracle. Maybe I was too critical. Maybe it looks okay on a larger scale. Maybe after washing or…maybe I've just accidentally taken a mood enhancing drug. It is horrible! I can hardly stand to look at it. So many hours and so much innocent fiber sacrificed on this piece. What am I going to do with it?

Usually I fold it up, stuff it in the back of a drawer or closet and try to forget about it. I don't know why (maybe it's that damn overactive character building gene again) but I've never been able to throw a failure away. Maybe like wine, a few years of aging will improve it. Perhaps moths will eat it and I won't feel so bad about throwing it away. Maybe when my emotions settle down, it won't be quite as painful to behold.

About a year ago I produced some yardage that went astray early on in the weaving process. I finished it because I felt sorry for the yards and yards of 5/2 pearl cotton and 2/8 wool that deserved better. When I confessed to a weaving friend how disappointed I was with my fabric, she asked if she could have it. Of course she could have it! I didn't even care or ask what she was going to do with it. She could cut it up and clean her bathroom with it. I would never have to look at it again. That was good enough for me.

Eventually my aesthetic pain subsided and I became curious as to why my friend wanted the ugliest thing I had ever woven. She is part of the NYC fashion industry and I briefly wondered if she had a special extrasensory design gene that enabled her to distill beauty from ugliness. This was a skill I definitely lacked. Was I missing out on some esoteric artistic ability?

It turns out I wasn't deficient in design genes. She took my weaving because it was ugly and therefore perfect for her upcoming fiber adventure. If you're a knitter, you've probably heard of yarn bombing or graffiti knitting, a colorful type of urban street art that doesn't require cans of spray paint. Knitters revel in wrapping unlikely objects such as fire hydrants, statues and lamp posts with knitted and crocheted covers. My fabric was scheduled to be wrapped around bits and pieces of New York City as part of an upcoming "handwoven" bombing. My weaving friend also plans to use my fabric for hang tags to promote fiber arts and her NY weaving guild.

Now instead of being hidden away in a dark place, my fabric will not only see the light of day but be part of a different artistic statement. Whew! It's a step up from being used to clean a bathroom.

# The Dream Machine

*I*t looks like a loom and sounds like a loom but it does more than weave threads together. As long as I'm not in a personal war zone battling threading errors or treadling mistakes, the rhythmic ballet of shuttle, beater and treadle seems to release my mind from everyday practicality. I may start off thinking about what to make for dinner, but after just a few minutes of weaving, involuntary daydreams always take over.

Unlike time machines crashing through time barriers at warp (I had to say it!) speed, I'm riding on a magic carpet in absolute silence. I gently float along in a reverie, exploring the quiet coves of my imagination. It's obvious that my practical side is not the captain of this voyage. Forget about meal planning; I am the star of daydream adventures as far-fetched as those in James Thurber's "The Secret Life of Walter Mitty."

Mr. Mitty saw himself as a big game hunter in Africa, among other heroic roles. What I imagine is equally ludicrous. I am mild mannered, humble and self-effacing, somewhat like a female version of Clark Kent. So how can I be having such bodacious dreams? Instead of being a big game hunter, I fantasize about becoming a big name writer. I start off with occasional small humorous pieces in my local newspaper. The public loves them and demands more. I get my own column which of course attracts the attention of other papers. From an article here and there, I become a nationally syndicated columnist. This is probably my favorite pipe dream because of all the delicious spin-off dreams it spawns. Before I know it, I'm on book tours, I'm a frequent guest on radio and television talk shows and the ultimate reward: "43 across; popular humorist." I'm a clue in *The New York Times* Sunday crossword puzzle.

These dream adventures amaze me. I'm fascinated as I sit on my magic carpet and watch the scenes unfold around me. Sometimes what's actually on my loom weaves its way into a daydream. It could be a scarf, baby blanket or even a dishtowel that becomes so sought after that I'm forced to go into production. This leads to forming my own company, which grows faster than Jack's beanstalk. Before long, Martha and I are good friends.

"And how long have you been having these dreams, Sherrie?" I'm sure a therapist would be able to trace this apparent need for grandiose success to some personality flaw, but I'm not looking for answers. Maybe the rhythm of weaving lulls the left side of my brain to sleep. "Party time!" yells the right side. Maybe I've found a trap door into a higher level of consciousness. Or maybe my loom has magic powers. We all know that in fairy tales, straw can easily be spun into gold, with a little help from Rumpelstiltskin. Unless he's planning to make a surprise visit to Whippany, NJ, I don't expect to produce golden cloth from 8/2 cotton. Instead my loom will continue to turn threads into dreams and I'll continue weaving my own fairy tales.

# UFOs in the Weaving Room

When my weaving friend started talking about her UFOs, it took me a few seconds to catch on. ET and his buddies hadn't popped in for an extraterrestrial visit. The UFOs she was referring to were her collection of "Unfinished Fiber Objects." Some of them had been living with her for a long time. She is not alone. We all have our own UFOs, some so old we've forgotten all about them. They usually show up by accident when we're looking for something else.

Most of my UFOs are at the bottom of baskets or at the back of drawers. Whatever frustration made me stop working on them was painful enough to make me want to hide them away, get them out of my sight. Seemingly simple, uncomplicated projects can be easily sabotaged by a variety of factors. I should have learned by now that most projects are not as simple or enjoyable as they first appear.

Eventually the inevitable build-up of UFOs started bothering me. On each New Year's Eve, I made the exact same resolution: "I will finish every abandoned project." This year was no different except that I really meant it this time. I had no choice. Every cabinet, bookcase, closet shelf, basket and plastic bin was stuffed beyond its storage capacity. The door on a cabinet wouldn't close anymore and the fronts and bottoms of several drawers kept falling apart.

Weavers are savers. That is a big part of the reason why we wind up working in jam-packed spaces. We never know what we'll need for a future project. To be safe, we simply hold onto everything. Our weaving rooms may look out of control but this is NOT to be confused with hoarding! We are artists.

I had crammed a lot in my little weaving room. If I ever wanted to buy another weaving book, have space for future *Handwoven Magazines*, or splurge on some exotic fiber, something had to go. Those bags of forsaken projects stuffed here and there were taking up a lot of valuable real estate. It was time to either throw them out or confront them and finish them. They were becoming an emotional burden and starting to weigh me down.

Clearing out clutter, on the other hand, has always given me an emotional boost. If cleaning out a closet or bookcase could make me feel energized, I knew that eliminating my fleet of UFOs would not only clean up my weaving room but cleanse my creative psyche. This time I was ready for action. Like a general planning a battle, I strategized about which UFO to attack first. Hidden away for years were unfinished mug rugs, still attached to their colorful popsicle stick loom, a half-finished coiled hot pad made of cotton cording wrapped in fabric strips, a dyed warp from a forgotten workshop, at least ten scarves waiting for their fringe to be twisted, a bag with balls of fluffy white mohair and a bungled unfinished mohair vest front still imprisoned on its knitting needles, and a half-knit oversized mitten waiting to be finished and felted. My rigid heddle loom still had the pick-up warp and weft sampler that Jane Patrick's book *Weaving on a Rigid Heddle Loom* had inspired me to start but never finish.

There was more. There was the yardage Daryl Lancaster had woven for me as part of our Jockey Hollow Weavers guild "potpourri" exchange. Our members had traded sealed bags of fiber. Out of my hodgepodge collection, Daryl had woven yards of a handsome fabric. It deserved better than to stand rolled up like a naughty child, collecting dust in a corner of my weaving room. And then there was the ultimate "souvenir" from my trip twelve years ago to the Isle of Harris off the northwestern coast of Scotland. One of the Outer Hebrides, this remote island is the home of the world renowned Harris Tweed weavers. I visited them and brought home four yards of iconic tweedy yardage. That small bolt of fabric deserved to be more than an occasional weaving show and tell.

I could hear every UFO calling out, "Finish me, finish me!" But where to start? To prove to myself that I was ready for this herculean task, I surveyed the choices. Some projects started smoothly enough and then hit glitches. Solving the problem that had derailed me would easily get me back on track. Other tasks like twisting or braiding fringe were just boring and time consuming. I decided to go with the most personally challenging project, the frustrating one that always left me feeling defeated. This was my "bête noire."

It was a small tapestry I enthusiastically started in 1998. In French, a bête noire is literally a "black beast" but my bête noire was actually a brown beast. It was a stylized image of a brown alpaca bordered by rows of zigzagging triangles. Every few years I had taken the tapestry out of the closet, always with renewed hope and good intentions. Each time it didn't take long for me to wind up cursing those intricate zigzagging shapes and shoving the tapestry back in the closet, far out of sight.

If I could finish this, I could finish anything. I even felt sorry for the little Beka frame loom, under tight warp tension without a break for the last fourteen years. Tapestry is slow-going and I'm slower than most weavers. So I knew this would take a long time. Always relating to that famous tortoise, I slowly moved forward. Inch by inch, week by week and little by little the alpaca took shape, surrounded by its pointy frame. And then one day it was done.

Like Aesop's Fables, there is a moral to my story. There is a prize for crossing a fiber finish line, but it's

not a trophy or a plaque. It's a joyous surge of pleasure combined with strong feelings of satisfaction
and achievement. I felt lighter and recharged, as if a
load had been lifted from my artistic soul. I don't
think I had ever felt so blissful about finishing a
piece of weaving before. And there was more bliss to
come with each UFO. I couldn't wait to shoot down
the next one.

# My Drug of Choice

$\mathcal{I}$t happened in Dora's driveway. Dora, a member of our Jockey Hollow Weavers guild, decided to sell off some of her stash, an impressive assortment of fiber collected over many weaving years. She had been storing everything in large plastic bins and wanted to sell those as well. To make it easy for us, she wrote our names on index cards and taped each of our names to a bin. All we had to do was drop the cones we wanted to buy into our own bin for safe-keeping. I admired her clever marketing technique.

She made it *too* easy. After a few minutes I realized my extra-large bin was overflowing with colorful cones piled high. I decided I needed a second bin. Her prices were ridiculously low. I kept grabbing more and more cones that I couldn't pass up. My face felt flushed and my heart was racing. I was high; high on fiber. When it looked like I would need to buy a third plastic bin, something made me stop. I had never felt this way before. What was going on? It took a minute to realize that I was out of control.

I was binging—not on alcohol or desserts, but on cones of fiber. Somehow I reached adulthood without ever feeling this way before. I didn't drink, smoke, buy shoes or collect anything. This was a new and unsettling experience for me. I thought about other weavers who told me they sneak fiber purchases into their homes so their husbands won't know they've been at it again. Now I understood what they were talking about. I was a fiber addict. My ratio of stash to storage space hadn't reached a critical level yet, but I was well on my way to achieving SABLE:    stash accumulation beyond life expectancy.

Was this really a bad thing? Weavers are artists who work with colored cones of fiber rather than tubes of paint. We can't create without supplies. So what's wrong with having as many different types, colors and sizes of fiber as possible? That was my philosophy for many years. I have pounds and pounds of souvenirs from that way of thinking. Many of those souvenirs have never left the shelves in my weaving room closet, since they were placed there at the end of the last millennium. Whatever creative inspiration was behind their purchase at WEBS, Rhinebeck Sheep and Wool or Shel. B. Small's Poughkeepsie, NY warehouse vanished years ago. Pity for these dusty, forgotten cones may finally inspire me to find a use for of them.

Now when I look at my hodgepodge collection of fiber, I wish I hadn't been such a weaving dilettante. Every time a *Handwoven Magazine* project caught my fancy, I just had to buy the appropriate materials. It's been a colorful ride collecting rayon chenille for all the shadow weave scarves I was sure I was going to make. And multiple tubes of carpet warp for all of the rep weave rugs I couldn't wait to make. I forget why I needed all of that Harrisville Shetland wool, but those heathery cones fill an entire plastic bin all by themselves.

It's the pearl cottons and the 8/2 unmercerized cotton that I turn to most often. Not exactly the plain-Janes of the fiber world, they certainly lack the glamour of today's fiber celebrities like bamboo, tencel and soy silk, the current superstars of our weaving universe. I've played with these flashy newcomers, but have always come back to my cotton cones. Cottons are dependable, versatile and have become my BFFFs: best fiber friends forever.

Every so often I will order a few new colors to round out the rainbow of cones of cotton lined up in my weaving room. That's the only safe way for me to buy fiber. Since that day in Dora's driveway when I first recognized that fiber was my drug of choice, I've learned how to manage my addiction. I must avoid being in direct contact with large quantities of yarn that's for sale. WEBS and Halcyon are too far away to be a problem, but there is danger lurking a mere 30 minutes away from me. It's called Silk City Fibers in Paterson, NJ.

Silk City Fibers bills itself as "the home of the world's finest yarns for designers and manufacturers." Monday through Friday, they sell wholesale to knitwear designers and production weavers, proudly stating on their website that they "offer thousands of colors in a multitude of yarn styles, all put up on cones for immediate delivery."

From Monday through Friday there's no problem. It's what happens during the four hours from 9:00 AM to 1:00 PM on the second Saturday of each month that I feel vulnerable. That's when they open to the public for retail sales. Haphazardly arranged in their retail outlet rooms are enough cones to keep every guild member in North America weaving for a very long time. Many are exotic yarns, like the cashmere/wool and the shetland/silk/cashmere/alpaca blends offered in last month's email flier. And these luxury fibers are usually on sale!

Seduced by their prices and selection, I gave into temptation and spent a few Saturday mornings at Silk City Fibers, merrily filling my shopping cart with irresistible bargains. Most of those bargains have never been used. After the experience in Dora's driveway it became obvious that I have no self-control when it comes to buying fiber. No matter how much I have it's never enough. I am a fiber addict. That's why Dora's driveway and Silk City Fibers are now permanently off-limits to me.

# Murphy's Law: The Fine Print

*D*id you know there is a special addendum to Murphy's Law that's just for weavers? Everyone knows that if something can go wrong it will. But not every weaver is aware of this addendum to Murphy's Law: the greater your need for a particular fiber, the more impossible it will be to find.

Our projects are conceived and designed with specific fibers. Last year I bought a ball of "Balu," a soft and silky cashmere/angora/acrylic blend. This luxurious white fluffy fiber was expensive, so I bought only one ball to experiment with. At the time I wanted to create fabric that looked like rabbit fur. This ethereal white ball already looked like a rabbit as I held it in my hand.

Designing fabric to look like a particular animal skin has always fascinated me. I've designed and constructed dinosaurs and mermaids with plaited twills, a weave structure resembling scales. I don't think of my woven creatures as stuffed animals. To me they really are soft sculptures. I try to imbue each one with a special essence, avoiding clichéd cuteness. When I bought that white fluffy fiber, there was a furry white rabbit hopping around in my mind.

That rabbit did become a reality, but without any help from that fluffy fiber. After sampling, it lost out to a cone of white eyelash, apparently the perfect fiber for weaving up faux rabbit fur. The rabbit that came from my fuzzy yardage had all the essence of rabbit I hoped to capture. But I kept what was left of that white ball of Balu next to my loom, knowing it would be perfect for something. And it was.

Using white Jaggerspun "Zephyr" (hideously expensive but worth it), I experimented with using short lengths of Balu to embellish a scarf. Weaving a basic 2/2 twill with the Zephyr, I placed a row of rya type knots across the width of the scarf every five inches for the entire woven length. After a gentle bath, this scarf was transformed into the softest fabric to ever come off my loom, with its rows of Balu fringe. When I wore that scarf one chilly winter night to a guild meeting, I knew I had come up with something special. That evening I presented a program on how to use handwoven fabric to make bags. I think my fellow guild members were interested in my topic. But when I asked if there were any questions, lots of hands went up and all their questions were about my scarf. What was it made from, how did I get that fringe and could I pass it around?

Having guild members, who've seen more scarves in their weaving careers than many French women in a lifetime, get excited about my scarf confirmed my belief that I had come up with a winner. This would be my prototype. With our annual guild sale still months away, I had enough time to weave more scarves.

Before I ordered more Zephyr, I decided to first buy some additional Balu. I could probably get two scarves from each ball. I went on-line to see who had the best price. Intending to buy six or so balls, it made sense to save money if possible. You probably know the rest of the story. There was no Balu to be found at any price anywhere. It had been sucked down a black hole. It had been discontinued!

Here was the fine print of Murphy's Law in action: Whatever fiber you desperately want, you will not find. If you don't really need something you will find it without a problem. A back-ordered yarn is almost as painful as a discontinued fiber. According to the yarn company's website, 59 of the 60 colors of the fiber type you need are available. A few satisfying clicks on the keyboard can deliver them to your mailbox in a days. But the one color you must have—the one color you can't continue your project without—is the only color in the entire line that's backordered.

Sometimes I understand why a color has sold out. What weaver couldn't use a little red or green before the holidays? Black, white and beige are also popular colors. They are like type O blood, compatible with every other color in a stash. I'm never surprised when they're on backorder, whether in cotton, silk or wool. What astonishes me is how that odd shade of moldy green I need, actually quite an unattractive color all by itself, can possibly be sold out. And you know if it's on backorder at one company, it's probably on backorder at the others. It's in a fiber state of limbo. You will eventually get your hands on it, but no one can tell you when.

So, desperate to continue your project, you turn to your stash. There must be something buried in one of those bins, dressers, baskets or closets that will work. Here's some more fine print from Murphy's Law that applies to all weavers: No matter how huge your stash you will not find what you need. You will find the right color in the wrong fiber or the right fiber in the wrong size. Worst of all, you may find exactly what you need but only a tiny bit of it, a left-over from a long-ago project.

Sooner or later the reality sinks in. Plan A is just not going to happen. It's time to rethink the project and work with what you have. Frustration turns into resignation and feelings of disappointment lead to a creative recklessness. If you can't carry out your perfect Plan A, it really doesn't matter what fiber you use. Now the goal is just to finish and move on. You're ready to try different colors and fibers.

A funny thing happens once you've opened your mind to new options. An unexpected color choice surprises you by actually looking better than that elusive original color. A spurt of excitement comes out of nowhere and draws you back into your project. You wonder why you didn't think of using this fiber before. Plan B is so much better than Plan A! Who could have predicted that the fine print in Murphy's Law would have such unanticipated advantages for weavers?

# The World's Most Famous Sweater

As an adult, weaving snuck up on me in the form of my Old English sheepdog, a dog with enough hair to regularly clog vacuum cleaners and create allergies in people who had never been allergic to anything in their lives. The handbook *How to Raise Your Old English Sheepdog* shows a photograph of a woman seated at a spinning wheel, surrounded by six enormous sheepdogs that slept as she spun their fluffy hair into yarn. I was living with a hair machine. I knew I had to learn to spin. Those never-ending tumbleweeds of sheepdog hair were more than just a messy embarrassing nuisance. They were a natural resource. Properly used, they could keep a family of four warm all winter.

Armed with a drop spindle, a pair of carders and *Spin Your Own Wool* by Molly Duncan, I attempted to transform my dog's downy hair into yarn. Simply brushing him provided an endless supply of fiber. I made a point to brush his grey and white areas separately. Whatever I ultimately made with his yarn would be in grey and white.

I wasn't a talented or even average spinner; I was awful at it. My drop spindle yarn at times was as fine as sewing thread and then mysteriously grew thick and lumpy. Thinking a spinning wheel would help, I bought a classic Ashford wheel which did make a difference. Now I could spin my highly irregular yarn a lot faster. Eventually my spinning ability did improve a little but I never felt totally in control. Over a long dark winter I brushed, carded and spun basketfuls of sheepdog hair into yarn. Sometimes I felt as if I had unknowingly traveled back in time. I was an alchemist of sorts, trying to transform dog hair into yarn, repeating to myself, "Hair today, yarn tomorrow."

It wasn't sorcery that transformed the fiber in my baskets into skeins of grey and white yarn. The idea of turning dog hair into usable yarn became more exciting with each newly spun skein and kept me permanently motivated. Eventually I realized that carding by hand was slowing me down. I advanced a few centuries by renting a drum carder, an invention that definitely belongs in the Spinning Hall of Fame. My production dramatically increased, filling my bobbins in half the time. I can't say I was becoming a better spinner, but I was going from dog hair brushings to finished plied skeins a lot more efficiently. Finally it was time to think about using my unique fuzzy grey and white stash. I decided to knit myself a sweater.

I hadn't knit since my childhood when my mother would cast on for me, find dropped stitches and fix my mistakes. My basic skills hadn't improved with time. Without my mother to guide me, I asked an acquaintance for some knitting advice. She was an experienced knitter who made up her own patterns and didn't think anyone needed a specific set of knitting instructions to make a simple sweater. Her advice sounded reasonable. She told me to measure how wide I wanted the sweater to be and then to cast on enough stitches to make the front and back that size. When I thought the front looked long enough I was supposed to decrease to make armholes. Making sleeves was equally simple: You just knit until they're long enough.

Following her advice without any printed instructions, I managed to knit a sweater back, front and two sleeves. My stitch repertoire was basic; I knew how to knit and purl and the only artistic license I took was to create a white stripe around the front, back and sleeves. Amazingly, the sweater actually fit.

This was not an ordinary sweater. It made a mohair or angora sweater look flat and had unexpected insulating properties. All that fluffy, fuzzy pile made the sweater warmer than any garment I had ever worn. If L.L.Bean had known about sheepdog yarn I bet it would have been rated superior to down. It was actually too hot to wear for very long. This was an extraordinary garment.

I was far from the first spinner to incorporate dog hair into yarn. Prehistoric Scandinavians made use of it. Native Americans combined it with wool from mountain goats and bark fiber to make blankets and clothing. Spinners have always used whatever fiber was available. Dog hair belongs on the list with sheep, llama, alpaca, camel, goat, musk ox and rabbit.

Whereas I saw my dog hair sweater in an historical and ecological perspective, my friends couldn't get past "she made it from her *dog's hair*." They thought my sweater was not only weird but somewhat creepy. They couldn't even look at it without making a face.

That sweater stole my identity. From then on I became known as "the woman who made a sweater from her dog's hair." That was how I was introduced at neighborhood parties. It was such a distinguishing fact that nothing I subsequently achieved would ever be impressive or interesting enough to replace the sweater story. I could have won a Nobel Prize, but even that accomplishment would have come in second to my sheepdog sweater.

It's been over 30 years since I made that sweater but when I run into someone from my old neighborhood now, I know exactly what they will say; "Aren't you the one who made that dog hair sweater?" It is an achievement that has become part of who I am. It also turns out to have been an unanticipated fiber milestone. After knitting the sweater, there was still a lot of sheepdog yarn left. My spinning skills hadn't improved much, nor had my knitting skills, although I became proficient at retrieving dropped stitches. I kept searching for something else to do with this exotic yarn.

And then I had a fiber epiphany. I remembered how much I loved weaving when I was eight years old. Why not weave with it? So, like so many other new weavers before and after me, I bought a Leclerc Dorothy table loom and Deborah Chandler's classic book *Learning to Weave*. Not trusting my uneven yarn to hold up under tension, I purchased some grey alpaca yarn for warp.

The marriage of sheepdog and alpaca yarn was a happy union. From this partnership came my first adult piece of weaving: a shawl for my Nana. Because she was my grandmother, she graciously accepted it and made no faces, at least not in front of me. This rustic and quirky textile was a personal tri-umph. I had read and reread Deborah Chandler's book so many times. I felt as if she was a guardian spirit, my fiber fairy godmother guiding and pro-tecting me from evil weaving gremlins. I've since met those demonic loom gremlins many times, but they were nowhere to be found as I warped and wove this mixed fiber grey and white shawl.

My second fiber epiphany appeared just a few weft shots later. An inch or so into my project, it became obvious: Weaving would now be an important part of my life. It made me feel happy. It still does.

# Craft Overload

*I* am an empty nester. My husband and I live in an average sized home. When my two sons left for good, I immediately reclaimed their former bedrooms and closets for my personal use. Empty nesters are supposed to talk about downsizing, but here I am fantasizing about upsizing, moving to a house with more space.

It's weaving that's the trouble maker, starting with my original LeClerc Dorothy table loom. That little loom along with its slim metal stand could be folded up and stored in a closet. But this loom had a secret dark side; it needed accessories and had an insatiable appetite for fiber. It quickly became obvious that its original 12 dent reed needed company and along came 8, 10 and 15 dent reeds. And then I had to have a boat shuttle. What weaver wouldn't spend a little money in pursuit of better selvedges? Of course, a boat shuttle needs a bobbin winder and it made sense to buy a cone stand, extra spools and a ball winder while I was at it.

By now my fiber collection filled all the drawers of what had been my son's dresser. The guest room closet became the home for my warping board. My guests were lucky to get a few inches of hanging space in-between the threatening pegs of the warping board and my own out-of-season clothes.

For a while I could hide everything in the guest room. Yardsticks, reeds, lease sticks, rolls of paper and corrugated cardboard happily collected dust and cat hair under the bed. Then spinning entered my world. No problem with my Ashford spinning wheel. It found a perfect home in a corner of the dining room. But like my Dorothy loom, it needed its own entourage of accessories. So now the reams of paper, labels and office supplies in my home office closet shared shelves with a wooden swift, niddy-noddy, lazy kate, bobbins, carders, drop spindles and a pungent bag of unwashed fleece.

Many scarves, dishtowels, place mats, runners and mug rugs later, when I found out I would become a grandmother, I bought a 36" Schacht Mighty Wolf floor loom. I thought I had entered the land of giants. Everything looked super-sized compared to the delicate proportions of my Dorothy loom. And since the Mighty Wolf had a mighty appetite for its own matching accessories, I found myself once again acquiring a set of reeds, but now they were all 36" long! My guest closet was looking as inviting as a torture chamber.

Belonging to a weaving guild is important to me. I can meet others with the same obsession and find inspiration and answers on the first Wednesday night of the month. But it's also dangerous, with all of those little workshops to introduce us to new related crafts. And all of those unfinished projects to bring home and store.

Whether I truly believe I will ever finish the decorative temari thread ball, the peyote stitch bead project, the Anni Albers metal washer/ribbon necklace, the tri-axial paper weaving, the coiled basket, the Chinese button ball and frog, the bobbin lace bookmark or the leaf-printed scarf isn't the issue. Of course I'll never finish these projects, but I can't just throw them out. That's why I drew the line at needle felting.

"Our January meeting will be a hands-on demonstration of needle felting. Be sure to bring an 8" square of extra dense foam rubber to the meeting." That's what the newsletter said. I should know because I'm the newsletter editor and even before I finished writing it I had made my decision. The door of my overstuffed guest room cabinet fell off last week and the night table drawer front was threatening to do the same. I had too much stuff jammed in them. A piece of foam rubber was the straw that broke the camel's back. NO MORE SUPPLIES! NO MORE CRAFTS! Not one more cubic inch would enter my house.

My plan was to be an observer at the meeting. I had seen needle felting demonstrated at our guild show. While I admired the finished creatures, especially a sporty fox one of our guild members had poked into life, I had no urge to play with barbed needles. If I was into piercing, my Toika temple would do the job. What an appropriate name for this tool with its needle-sharp teeth. Every time I use it I sacrifice some blood.

"And who needs a piece of foam rubber? I've brought some extras for you." That's all it took. How could I disappoint this enthusiastic, well prepared woman? So I paid the $5 material fee and in return received a starter set of felting needles and a piece of foam rubber to rest my project on.

Put a tool in my hand and I go into autopilot. Now that I owned these needles of course I had to use them. By the end of the meeting I had needle felted a plump red heart with white trim to give to my husband for Valentine's Day. I was flattered when the instructor took a picture of it. Red fleece was a good color choice; my blood stains didn't show.

But this is absolutely *the last* craft supply I will bring home.

# Draftlexia

*I* should hang my college diploma up as a reminder that I graduated from college Magna Cum Laude. Back then this didn't seem so remarkable to me. Other than a slap in the face from high school chemistry, I dutifully paid attention in all of my classes, took notes, studied for tests and usually got As.

And then I discovered weaving. I was determined to learn more about it. Not knowing any real-life weavers, I bought Deborah Chandler's classic *Learning to Weave*. It became my Weaving 101 textbook. Deborah's friendly approach made me feel as if she was sitting next to me guiding me along. I treated each of her chapters as a lesson and wove different samplers from her list of homework assignments to test my new knowledge.

Warping seemed scary at first, but by reading the steps over and over (and over and over), I managed to tame an angry warp into submission. I worked my way to "Part 3: For Those of You Who Know What you're Doing." I was sure that included me. How proud I was of my "Chapter 10: Double Weave" sampler with every option Deborah mentioned in her double weave draft. This was a personal tour de force. Drunk with power, I kept switching layers, making closed tubes and ending with a double width section. Many weaving years later, I still feel happy when I look at this little woven piece.

Next came "Lesson 11: Honeycomb," followed by "Lesson 12: Loom Controlled Lace Weaves." No problems there. I understood weaving drafts by then, although I often had to stop, close my eyes, and think about which warp ends were up and which were down. Something I still do today.

And then came "Lesson 13: Block Theory," and along with it some previously unknown mental blocks of my own. To explain profile drafts, Deborah uses the block pattern of a moose head. I studied that moose pattern over and over, trying to understand the relationship of the blocks to that simplified moose head. For a while I even thought the staggered blocks were the moose legs and feet. Every so often the veil of mystery would lift and I'd start to see the logic behind those blocks. But the next time I confronted the moose, the logic of it all had faded away. This was the first time and certainly not the last time I felt humbled by weaving. It appears that I have previously undiagnosed learning disabilities that only apply when warp and weft are involved. I have "draftlexia."

That moose haunted me for a long time. Every so often I would revisit it. Many projects later, I finally grasped the concept of a profile draft. Those weren't moose legs and feet after all, just part of the profile draft. Finally I could move past Lesson 13.

After my block theory breakthrough, I regained weaving self-confidence and made good friends with Summer and Winter, an orderly weave structure that made perfect sense to me. With eight shafts to play with, I could bring graph paper doodles to life on my loom. Picasso had his "Blue Period" and I had my "Animal Period," transforming graph paper dogs, cats, fish and dinosaurs into woven cloth. It was always satisfying to see pattern wefts slowly turn into the shapes I had drawn on graph paper.

My self-confidence didn't last long. It was at a weaving workshop that I had a draftlexia relapse. The initial weaving drafts presented by the instructor were understandable and I grasped the concepts behind them, at least for a while. And then things got murky, very murky, and I gave up trying to make sense of the Fiberworks drafts projected on the wall. The rest of the workshop members kept nodding their heads in enthusiastic appreciation as the instructor continued her presentation. Instead I began to notice that many of the drawdowns looked like animal skins. If I ever wanted to make a giraffe, a leopard or a zebra, here were the perfect weaving drafts to get spots, curving stripes and interesting blotches. I reviewed the instructor's handout several times after the workshop, hoping for another break-through, but never had that "eureka!" moment. Many workshops later there is no denying I have a disability. I am draftlexic.

It's at workshops that my fiber limitations become apparent. Following a weaving draft is never a prob-lem, but understanding the theory behind a weaving structure is my downfall. I've played with twills, overshots, lace weaves, rep weaves, even mind-bog-gling double weave pick-up, but still can't explain what makes most of them work. The weaving sector of my brain is like a calculator that can't compute anything that requires more than four digits. I remember being astonished to learn that overshot is actually a block weave.

I briefly thought about enrolling in the "Certificate of Excellence" program sponsored by the Handweavers Guild of America. This rigorous and terrifying certificate program would be like marine boot camp for me. No doubt I would have many eureka moments, but they would come along with emotional suffering and frequent meltdowns. Other than my cat, no one would be able to stand me.

Having huge gaps in my understanding of weaving theory hasn't had a negative affect on my love for weaving. Instead it has continued to fill me with amazement. Not knowing exactly how a magic trick is done adds to its enjoyment. The same applies to weaving. I don't have to understand the theory behind a draft to appreciate it. Sometimes it just feels good to believe in magic.

MILLER
& HILL

# *Fringe Benefits*

*I*t was the news that I would be a first-time grandmother that made me decide to buy a floor loom. Up until then I was happy with my Leclerc Dorothy table loom. My weaving horizon was never wider than 15 ¾″ and that was fine with me. A constant flow of ideas for scarves, place mats, towels and runners kept my loom in production. Who knows? Perhaps I would still be pressing those colorful metal levers today without the advent of grandchildren.

My future granddaughter needed a proper baby blanket. For the first time in my weaving career, 15 ¾″ just wasn't wide enough. A new 36″ Schacht Mighty Wolf floor loom entered my life a month before my first granddaughter. I christened my loom by weaving a soft cotton baby blanket, which I named "the world's most expensive blanket," factoring in its cost along with the Monte Cristo textured cotton that I used. My blanket was appreciated and used, but along the way it was a green L.L.Bean fleece blanket that became her "can't-sleep-without" security blanket.

A few years later when her baby sister was born, I used Bernat's Cottontots to weave an equally soft blanket. I finished it with twisted fringe, as I had with the first blanket. My family lives about four and a half hours away, so I didn't get to see my grandchildren as often as I would have liked. I hoped the blanket was being used.

The answer was "yes." Not only was the blanket being used, but my new granddaughter "needed it" at all times. My daughter-in-law was finding it hard to get it away long enough to wash it. Could I please weave a second blanket? Could I do it quickly? If ever there was a weaving SOS, this was it. After a quick trip to Michaels for some more hanks of Cottontots and a couple of days of non-stop warping and weaving, I put a duplicate blanket in the mail.

During visits it was obvious that my blankets were loved; my granddaughter had one of them with her at all times. When she was around two years old I received another weaving SOS. "Wherever we go, the blanket comes with us. She's dragging it along sidewalks and filthy parking lots. It's really too big to take on outings. Could you possibly make some smaller on-the-go versions?"

Never had any weaving customer so appreciated my textiles. Back to Michaels for more yarn. A few days later I mailed several 12 x 18" portable versions of the original blanket. By now my granddaughter was old enough to talk about her blankets, so I asked why she liked them so much. Was it because I wove them out of plushy soft cotton, or was it the pastel log cabin design that intrigued her? Her answer surprised me: "Grandma, I like the fringe." The twisted fringe was the best part of the blankets. Playing with the fringe brought her happiness and I understood perfectly. (See "My True Confession.")

The blanket saga didn't stop there. She wanted her dolls and stuffed animals to have their own fringed blankets. Out of some leftover yarn, I needle-wove a few miniature blankets on a Fast Sam (a gadget to try out setts before warping a loom). With twisted fringe, of course. There was still a little more weaving to be done. Eventually the fringe wore out on one of the original blankets and a very familiar pastel log cabin pattern once again took shape on my loom. It's incredibly satisfying to know that my weaving has brought my granddaughter so much contentment and happiness. Now that she's growing up, I've decided if she ever needs a new blanket, I'll teach her how to weave one herself.

# Not Just a Dishtowel

"*D*ishtowels? Why in the world are you bothering to go to all of this fuss to weave dishtowels?" This was a reasonable question from my husband. He had walked away in disbelief, actually shaking his head as he watched me try to tame angry snarls that were once orderly warp chains. Threading errors, sleying errors, broken warp threads—this project had them all. Why put forth such effort for the sake of a lowly dishtowel when I could buy one at the supermarket for $1.89? Why bother?

I was asking myself the same question. A picture of this thick and thin log cabin pattern with its tricky arrangement of broken stripes had long intrigued me. Plus it required only two harnesses. A great project for a beginner, I thought. The thick warp was a lovely pearl cotton which behaved itself. The thin warp was white sewing thread—2,000 yards of it—which seemed to resent being used for weaving. Once off its spool, the sewing thread showed its anger by instantly snarling up into a tangled mess.

Detangling, threading and sleying took hours and hours. My eyes could hardly focus on the thread or the 15 dent reed. Since the sleying directions were complicated, I of course made many mistakes. Was any dishtowel worth so much time and frustration? Why not just quit and save the remaining pearl cotton for a less grim project?

I couldn't quit. At first I thought it was plain stubbornness that kept me at the loom, a dogged determination fanned by pride. But after much thought, I began to understand why I had to keep going. Every weaving project has its own validity and importance. The clever threading that produces this complex design on only two shafts is fascinating, as is the use of thick and thin threads together in a log cabin pattern. Using this pattern for dishtowels instead of a table runner or tablecloth doesn't diminish its validity. I had to complete them.

Even the most utilitarian items can have beautiful designs, workmanship and personal significance. The ordinary can be exceptional. Instead of being saved and brought out for special occasions, these dish towels will bring me enjoyment every day.

Among my favorite family heirlooms are my mother's old wooden rolling pin and her colorful mixing bowls, homey reminders of everyday life. I wonder if my children will feel the same about these blue and white dishtowels.

# Death, Taxes and Mistakes

Whoever said the two things you can always count on are death and taxes was wrong. My list includes one additional constant: mistakes. No matter how careful I think I am, I can always count on making at least one weaving mistake that remains invisible to me until I cut my piece off the loom. Some goofs are fairly easy to fix, but others are there forever.

It's always the same emotional script. *Satisfaction.* I'm finished at last. Days, weeks or months of work are over and something wonderful is waiting for me in the secret roll at the front of my loom. *Anticipation.* I unroll the new cloth. *Happiness.* What a wonderful idea I had! Those colors did work well together after all. And then the inevitable. *Despair.* Oh, no. How did I ever miss this mistake?

I have the same conversation with myself each time I discover one. How could I have not seen this obvious mistake? Wasn't I paying attention? If only I had seen it a row or two after it happened. Where was my mind? I know where it was: probably guarding the selvedges, protecting them from excessive draw-in or concentrating on keeping an even beat.

Sometimes mistakes can be selling features. We've all bought items of clothing that came with prominent tags bragging about their irregular weave or coloring. "These are not defects," the tags try to convince us. "These are the signs of handmade fabric and you are obviously discriminating enough to appreciate this fabric more than some boring perfectly woven machine-made version."

If someone else has woven a piece with mistakes, I can be accepting. An art teacher once pointed out that the "irregularity" of a piece of art could actually be what makes it special. The mother of a Navajo boy I sponsored through Children, Inc. once sent me a small woven rug as a thank you present. The brown, black and white wool was spun from the fleece of her family sheep on the Navajo reservation in Arizona. My art teacher was right. It's because of all the symmetrical irregularities of its design that I love this little rug. If I had woven the rug, I wouldn't be able to look at its misshapen geometry without wincing. I couldn't keep it in the same room with me.

My weaving rejects fall into three categories. A few pieces are so personally offensive that I have to get them out of my sight. They would be eternal reminders of wasted time and money and would keep me from weaving anytime soon. Then there's the group that I half believe I will use in a mutated form one day. Maybe sections could be salvaged for pockets or bands on future projects. I ignore the fact that I know this will never happen.

The last group includes borderline successes. The original concept was OK, but something happened along the way. These are the most frustrating pieces of weaving because they could have been really nice if only I hadn't made some careless mistakes. They are constant reminders of my emotional relationship with weaving. "Why do you even bother?" they silently ask. How to get rid of the evidence of my incompetency? Sell them! Sell them cheap!

I'm so grateful for our guild's annual fall show and sale at a local community center in Brookside, NJ. When a crowd of shoppers is standing outside on a cold November morning waiting for doors to open, you know there's a strong market for handwoven goods. This is a good thing. We are all happy to reinvest our profits into new fiber to start the cycle once again. Remember the water cycle we learned as kids? For weavers it's fiber instead of rain that keeps the cycle going. Buy fiber, weave stuff, sell stuff, buy more fiber and repeat over and over again.

I look forward to this annual sale. It's my way of getting rid of pieces that have mistakes. To my ever supportive husband these pieces always look fine. He tells me that I'm being too critical and that nobody else would ever notice or care about such minor, practically invisible flaws. All I can see are the mistakes glaring back at me in defiance. Some visitors to our annual guild show and sale have gotten bargains. My pricing depends on whether I can stand looking at something for another year. Really low pricing can keep a chenille scarf with a few treadling mistakes from going back home with me at the end of the day. I wonder if the woman who bought my blue and purple scarf with the narrow green stripes ever wondered why it was half the price of the other scarves. The opposite also happens when I am emotionally attached to something I wove. For several years I brought a small chenille pillow to our yearly sale. It didn't go with anything in my house but it was so cute I priced it ridiculously high to keep it from selling. Each year I watched people pick it up and admire it, but the price tag made them put it down again. Finally I got tired of carrying it back and forth, priced it fairly and sold it right away.

Every year as our sale approaches, the art of properly pricing handwovens becomes a hot topic. The general consensus is that some guild members are under pricing their work, which cheapens the value of handwovens for everyone. I sit quietly because I know I'm guilty. But I have my own rationale. By offering pieces for bargain prices, I'm allowing more of the public to acquire handwoven textiles. I'm not a traitor to weavers everywhere. I'm a weaving missionary!

# Finding the perfect loom

*I* think it's easier to find Nemo than to find the perfect loom. Why? Because there is no such thing as the perfect loom. We think there is but it's a myth. When we buy our first loom, we're all sure we've made the right choice. We've chosen a partner and expect to weave happily ever after.

Sadly, like a honeymoon, loom contentment doesn't last forever. Issues arise and they're always the fault of the loom. *Handwoven Magazine* is an instigator, always tempting us with projects that need more shafts or a wider weaving width than we have. When I was ready to buy my first loom, like many other beginning weavers, I decided on the ever-popular four shaft Leclerc Dorothy. I bought Marguerite P. Davison's classic book *A Handweaver's Pattern Book* and was astounded by the awesome power of a four shaft loom. If my Dorothy and I were capable of weaving the dazzling "Lee's Surrender" overshot pattern (page 184), what more could I ever want from a loom?

If you're a weaver, you've probably already guessed that there was a lot more I eventually wanted from my first loom. I'm sure there are weavers out there who have made king size coverlets from lengths of 15 3/4" Dorothy yardage. There's probably even a weaver bride who coaxed a stunning wedding gown from her little loom. These are the weaving rock stars, the gold medal winners of a weaving Olympiad. Yes, I know about double weave/double width, but I never could tame that telltale fold line or accept double weave's four shaft pattern limitations. So after being happily married to my Dorothy for about five years, I started flirting with the idea of purchasing a new loom.

Loom shopping is a lot harder than car shopping. Loom dealers are not conveniently clustered up and down our highways like car dealers. (If only!)Test driving a loom is often impossible unless you happen to live near a weaving center that carries the brand and model you're interested in. Some European brands have very limited distribution. If you don't have a weaving buddy who by luck owns the exotic imported loom that's caught your eye, you're forced to trust internet scuttlebutt.

My search for a Dorothy replacement led me to a mainstream loom. Out of the handful of weavers I knew at the time, several owned Schacht looms and they all gave me a thumbs-up for the Wolf models. The Spinnery, one of the few weaving stores in NJ, actually had a Schacht floor loom on display. Watching the owner demonstrate how easy it was to tie up the treadles was all it took to win me over. The Mighty Wolf looked like a Dorothy on steroids with its 36″ width and impressive eight shaft lineup but it still looked user-friendly. Here was a loom for the mechanically challenged. I bought it.

After a few practice projects I was prepared for the big time. OK *Handwoven*, bring it on! Now I'm ready for your eight harness shadow weave, color-and-weave pinwheels and lively block twills. I've escaped from my 15 ¾″ prison and can't wait to revel in the expansive freedom of my 36″ stainless steel reed.

The Mighty Wolf was a great choice for my "move up" loom. Eight shafts and the 36″ reed potential was an intoxicating combination. As a weaving dilettante I wove whatever took my fancy and bounced from rep weave rugs to lacey linen curtains. For a while I was on Daryl Lancaster's Fashion Forecast team and wove yardage to create garments using her color palettes for *Handwoven* articles. For fourteen years I had what I thought was the perfect loom.

The troublemaker was a stegosaurus dinosaur. I enjoyed doodling on graph paper and quickly realized that the more detailed the design, the more blocks and shafts you need to weave the image. Summer and Winter is my favorite block structure, but an eight harness loom will give you only six blocks to play with. (Shafts one and two are for tie down threads.) When you're trying to create a weaving draft for a playful dinosaur, a mere six blocks doesn't allow for important details like a pointy back. For the first time I felt "shaft-deprived." I needed more harnesses to bring my graph paper doodles to woven life. I actually began toying with the idea of buying another loom, a mega multi-harness model.

Multi-shaft floor looms come with multi-dollar price tags. I just couldn't justify the expense or imagine where I would put one. Does anyone really need eight looms? Why couldn't I be satisfied with my five Voyageur table looms, Mighty Wolf floor loom and Glimakra rigid heddle loom? Wasn't I the one who bragged about how good it felt to get rid of stuff? Maybe this was just a passing whim. If I waited long enough, perhaps it would go away. I had bought used cars for less than the cost of these looms.

Those budget-busting prices didn't stop me from online window shopping. Over a few months I became quite familiar with the name brand multi-shaft floor loom market. The stratospheric prices of the computer controlled looms, plus the fear of cranky over-heated solenoids, kept me from even considering one. A low-tech mechanical dobby loom, too old-fashioned for many weavers, seemed like the right choice for me. Even though I had no intention of buying a new loom I still day-dreamed about one of them: a Louet Magic Dobby 24 shaft loom.

It was an email that unexpectedly turned my day dreams into reality. A weaver in Pennsylvania wanted to sell one of her looms. I had to read the email twice to be sure I was reading it correctly. Yes, there it was: a Louet Magic Dobby 24 shaft loom for sale in the next state! The owner said it was in excellent condition and offered it to me at an extremely reasonable price. My husband and I drove out to get it the next day.

Now that I own eight looms (this is absolutely the last loom I will ever buy!) I've come to realize that while there's no such a thing as a perfect loom, a weaver can still find loom perfection. All it takes is finding the perfect *group* of looms.

# Warning:
## Weaving May Be Addictive

*A*s a weaver I have this extra sense, a form of radar that's always on, constantly scanning my field of vision for interesting incoming textiles. I wish I could turn it off, but it's an involuntary system that I don't seem to have any control over. And it can get me in trouble.

As I made my weekly shopping tour up and down the aisles of my local Pathmark supermarket one fall afternoon, I saw a woman. She was an elderly woman (this means anyone who I think looks older than me), wearing a simple jacket made from a really fabulous material. I wondered if she had any idea that her nubby bouclé jacket in dark reds, purples and blues would be the highlight of any weaving convention. My personalized jacket pattern from Daryl Lancaster's workshop has been waiting for such a deserving fabric.

She was walking with another woman, and the two of them were intently chatting together in a foreign language I couldn't identify. I hoped it would keep her from noticing me staring at that jacket. I'm not an intuitive weaver. To understand the structure of anything but tabby or a simple twill fabric, I definitely have to devote serious time to a piece of graph paper. But at least I could try to get an up close and personal look.

Following her at a discrete distance didn't help. I just had to get closer. At guild meetings it's acceptable to greet members by touching, stroking or patting whatever handwoven they're wearing. It's even a compliment to have someone go straight for your neck to touch the hot-off-the-loom scarf that you've brought for show and tell. Weavers seem to have an inherent right to touch textiles that other weavers are wearing. Could I accidentally brush up against her?

She suddenly turned around and stared back at me. Maybe I was following her too closely. I smiled and feigned great interest in the olive oils she was standing next to. She shook her head. Even though she spoke in a foreign language, I knew she was talking about me to her friend. I snuck a last peek as she lost no time heading away from that "crazy woman." I'm lucky she didn't complain to the manager. I can see the headline: "Woman questioned in bizarre stalking incident."

Whether I'm watching a movie, news or even a commercial on television, I'm involuntarily hard-wired to the textile alarm. It happened again last night. While watching an episode of *As Time Goes By* on TV, a British import with Judy Dench and Jeffrey Palmer, my radar picked something up. There it was:  a long beige and brown scarf wrapped around the house-keeper's neck. I'll have to catch a repeat to see how the episode ended, because I became fixated on that patterned scarf. The brain cells specializing in weaving automatically took command. Instead of following the story, I found myself following its design.

Being a weaver has definitely altered the world as I perceive it. My radar scope responds to all media. Pillsbury roll and biscuit commercials are sources for interesting placemats and bread cloths. Catalogs from Crate & Barrel, Williams Sonoma and Martha Stewart are my personal inspiration sources for sophisticated color combinations and great dish-towel ideas.

My husband has also developed his own specialized form of weaving radar. He had his weaving con-sciousness raised when my 36" floor loom arrived with "some assembly required." While I am fine-tuned to the textiles themselves, his system now picks up all examples of the weaving process. He's a "loom" man.  He has found looms and weaving scenes in more movies than you would ever imagine. If I'm not watching with him, he tapes every instance to show me later. Just last night he found a few seconds of card weaving in *The Iron Age*, a reality show that stripped modern man of the last 1000 years of human progress for our viewing pleasure. His tracking system remains set on full power, even when reading. Here's a newspaper headline that caught his eye one morning: "Malpractice bill debate stalls as doctors' slowdown looms." This was obviously a false alarm.

In Betty MacDonald's wonderful book *The Egg and I*, her humorous account of life on a chicken ranch, word got out that she enjoyed reading. So some of her well-meaning neighbors saved old newspapers for her to read. Ever since word got out that I am passionate about weaving, I couldn't ask for a more efficient volunteer news clipping service. My friends and family keep me updated on every weaving and spinning demonstration or exhibition. Visitors to all parts of England manage to come back with pictures of a weaver's cottage in whatever village they visited.

Here's a test to determine whether or not you've been "warped" by weaving:

Have you ever tried to identify the string of your tea bag? Tetley Tea uses a really nice string...could it be an 8/2 cotton?

Have you ever found yourself studying the upholstery fabric on your airline seat? My flight to France last fall definitely seemed to go faster.

Have you ever counted threads instead of sheep? When I can't fall asleep, I depend on my self-generating sleep aid: I try to create a weaving draft in my head. This tedious exercise works better than warm milk for me.

Do you ever get more excited about the packing material than the item you ordered? A tall wooden plant stand came wrapped in a long roll of 36" wide corrugated cardboard. The stand was pretty nice, but that cardboard has become my favorite warp thread separator.

Are men's plaid shirt patterns more interesting to you than the men wearing them? Maybe if I were younger and single my answer would be different, but there are enough different men's shirt patterns to create a definitive *Book of Men's Shirt Plaids* to keep next to your copy of Marguerite Davidson's *A Handweaver's Pattern Book*.

If you had one "yes" answer, you have managed to stay in "the normal person" zone. Two or more "yes" answers, and you're definitely warped. Five "yes" answers? You may wonder, as I do, whether weaving is an addiction or a hobby.

WEAVING
HALL OF
FAME

# The Weaving Hall of Fame

*I*'ve always felt a real debt to the great minds of the ancient world. Without their understanding of the nature of things, I wouldn't have figured out even the most basic concepts. The sun comes up and goes down, so it must be going around us. Thank you, Copernicus, for proving otherwise.

I feel the same debt of gratitude to the great weaving minds that came before me. If I had been a prehistoric weaver, I would have spent my entire weaving life picking my way row by row, like children still do today on their potholder looms, patiently going over and under each warp end.  If that's what had been passed down, I would have dutifully continued the tradition, Maybe, just maybe, I would have figured out on my own how to raise all the even or odd warps in one motion with sticks or string. But that one innovation would have been the only creative highlight of my weaving lifetime.

It's probably because of my complete lack of mechanical skills that I am so grateful to our pioneering weavers, many from prehistory. Unlike today's textile gods and goddesses, they will never receive the glory they deserve for inventing new structures or techniques. Today we take our anonymous ancestral weavers for granted. They never wrote monographs or taught workshops, but their contributions to our weaving world are immeasurable. It's time to pay homage to these forgotten weaving trailblazers from past millennia. While we're at it, we should also recognize and honor some of our contemporary fiber trailblazers. It's time to establish a Weaving Hall of Fame. Here are my nominations:

<u>Twisted cords</u>
When I show my beginning weaving students how to twist fringe, they are always amazed. Who would expect that two separate cords twisted in the same direction, when joined would energetically twist together in the opposite direction, creating a decorative spiral? This discovery allowed spinners to keep a newly spun yarn from untwisting by plying it with a second yarn spun in the same direction. Weaving as we know it wouldn't have been possible without this monumental fiber discovery. So the earliest makers of plied string from at least 15,000 years ago deserve to be the first admission to the Weaving Hall of Fame.

## The multi-shaft loom

What an ingenious invention! For thousands of years weaving didn't dramatically change. Whether weavers worked on upright, ground or backstrap looms, their looms had basically two sheds or spaces between the upper and lower warp yarns for the weft to travel. When even numbered threads were raised, the odd numbered threads were lowered and vice versa. That type of weaving is known as plain weave or tabby. Even within this limitation early weavers found ways to create patterns and designs. I like to imagine introducing a Neolithic weaver to a modern four-shaft loom. What a mind-blowing invention for a New Stone Age weaver. We take multi-harness looms for granted, but the invention of a four-shaft loom, modest by today's standards, was revolutionary. The multi-shaft loom and its visionary inventor belong in the Weaving Hall of Fame.

## The invention of twill.

Creating diagonal lines was genius. You could control whether they sloped up to the right or the left. Did early weavers immediately see how exciting this new direction was? Or did the conservative ones (I'm afraid I might have been one of the diehards) complain that those diagonal lines were messing up their perfectly straight grids?

## Double Weave

The 10 inch wide sampler I show my weaving students has a surprise. The top of it looks like an orderly piece of weaving with examples of tabby, basket weave, twill, and rib weave. It's the bottom half that astonishes my students the first time they see it and leaves then wide-eyed. Instead of being a single layer of fabric like the top half, it opens up like a book with a fold at the middle. It just doesn't seem possible. How could a flat 10 inch wide piece of weaving suddenly become 20 inches wide, twice the width of the top half?

Even though I've woven double weave in all its forms, I've never stopped marveling at what still seems to be a weaving miracle. With just a 4-shaft loom you can create cloth twice the loom's width, create open or closed tubes and playfully switch top and bottom layers of weaving on a whim. What an innovation! To the unknown weaving wizard who figured out how to harness the power of 4 shafts to create double weave, we salute you!

The floating selvedge

The floating selvedge is simple and brilliant at the same time. Instead of just settling for the fact that certain weave structures don't always catch the selvedge warp ends, some imaginative weaver dreamt up the idea of a floating selvedge. Bravo for this brainstorm.

The cross

When demonstrating how to measure out warp on a warping board, my new weaving students always ask why they have to bother making a cross. Wouldn't it be easier to make straightforward trips up to the top peg and back down to the bottom peg without fussing over that annoying cross? It's only when they begin sleying and threading their warp that the value of a cross becomes apparent. Whether a warp has 100 or 1,000 ends, that simple cross keeps everything in order. Without a cross, there would be chaos in the weaving room. This little step on a warping board is a giant step for weavers everywhere.

## McMorran's Yarn Balance

The first time one sees a McMorran Yarn Balance in action, it's hard to believe that such a seemingly simple device can calculate the yards per pound of any fiber. This measuring tool takes the mystery out of mystery yarns. A quick Google search tracked down the real Mr. McMorran of yarn balance fame. He was a former lecturer in textile testing at the Scottish College of Textiles in Galashiels, Scotland. It's time to honor him as a modern day nominee. Unfortunately this clever gadget is no longer being made, but that doesn't diminish its genius. Welcome, Mr. McMorran! You definitely belong in the Weaving Hall of Fame.

So I officially induct these fiber superheroes to the Weaving Hall of Fame. Their original contributions to our craft deserve formal recognition. "If I have seen further, it is by standing on the shoulders of giants." This familiar expression was found in the letters of Isaac Newton. He was referring to the great scientists who came before him and laid the groundwork for his own scientific discoveries. Through the Weaving Hall of Fame, I am giving credit to some of the fiber giants who came before me.

I like to imagine myself going back in time, even back into prehistory, to watch the fiber story slowly unfold. Would today's weavers feel a bond with our early weaving ancestors? Does a love for fiber transcend millennia? I would like to think that we would be kindred spirits, united by the universal frustration of a broken warp end or a glaring threading error.

It's traveling into the fiber future that's harder for me to imagine. When I bought my Schacht Mighty Wolf in 1998, I initially felt intimidated by its 8 shafts. Now there are 24 shafts waiting to be called into action on my Louet Magic Dobby loom and that's not really such an impressive number anymore. Even the basic Leclerc Dorothy, a starter loom for so many of us, can be ordered these days with as many as 12 shafts.

I felt so empowered when I first learned how to read a weaving draft. With just a pencil and piece of graph paper I could do drawdowns and bring drafts to life. Today all it takes is choosing one of the many computer weaving programs available to weavers. Endless threading, tie-up and treadling options are just a click away.

It's impossible to miss the dramatic fiber revolution. Does your stash include Bambu, Tencel or Soysilk? How about a cone of silk-wrapped stainless steel? The cosmetic industry touts seaweed as a skin moisturizer and now there's a fiber made from seaweed and silk. For the electronically advanced there are fiber optic threads to add that extra spark of excitement to projects.

When I was growing up computers were omnipotent machines. They appeared in science fiction movies and documentaries about what the future held. Their enormous size and weight (Univac 1 weighed 29,000 pounds with 5,200 vacuum tubes!) were awe-inspiring. Somehow when I wasn't looking, greatly scaled down models, mere shadows of their Univac and Eniac parents, found their way into our homes. They rapidly became part of our everyday lives and now we need them to work and play. Some weavers need them to weave.

If all of these changes could happen in just a few short decades, how can we even guess what our weaving future holds? Will our current crop of looms eventually be displayed in museums as quaint antiques, like spinning wheels from bygone times? Will our handwoven textiles of today be revered as much as the embroidered samplers of past centuries? The answers to these questions lie beyond our horizon.

I would like to think that as long as there is some version of a loom and some fiber to work with, there will always be weavers. Perhaps someday these future weavers will look back with historical nostalgia and nominate my Louet 24-shaft Magic Dobby loom for induction into the Weaving Hall of Fame.